EUROPE

by Claire Vanden Branden

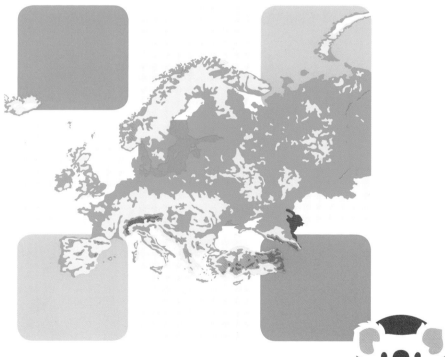

Cody Koala

An Imprint of Pop!

popbooksonline.com

abdobooks.com
Published by Pop!, a division of ABDO, PO Box 398166, Minneapolis,
Minnesota 55439. Copyright © 2019 by POP, LLC. International copyrights
reserved in all countries. No part of this book may be reproduced in any
form without written permission from the publisher. Pop!™ is a trademark
and logo of POP, LLC!.

Printed in the United States of America, North Mankato, Minnesota.

092018
012019

THIS BOOK CONTAINS
RECYCLED MATERIALS

Cover Photo: Shutterstock Images
Interior Photos: Shutterstock Images, 1, 5 (top), 5 (bottom left), 6, 7, 11, 13, 14,
15, 17, 18, 20, 21; iStockphoto, 5 (bottom right); Red Line Editorial, 8
Editor: Charly Haley
Series Designer: Laura Mitchell

Library of Congress Control Number: 2018949681
Publisher's Cataloging-in-Publication Data
Names: Vanden Branden, Claire, author.
Title: Europe / by Claire Vanden Branden.
Description: Minneapolis, Minnesota: Pop!, 2019 | Series: Continents |
    Includes online resources and index.
Identifiers: ISBN 9781532161735 (lib. bdg.) | ISBN 9781641855440 (pbk) |
    ISBN 9781532162794 (ebook)
Subjects: LCSH: Europe--Juvenile literature. | Continents--Juvenile literature.
    | Geography--Juvenile literature.
Classification: DDC 940--dc23

Hello! My name is

Cody Koala

Pop open this book and you'll find QR codes like this one, loaded with information, so you can learn even more!

Scan this code* and others like it while you read, or visit the website below to make this book pop.

popbooksonline.com/europe

*Scanning QR codes requires a web-enabled smart device with a QR code reader app and a camera.

Table of Contents

Chapter 1

Europe

Europe is a small **continent**.
It has 50 countries. Some are
partly in Asia, such as Russia.

Europe and Asia are
a **landmass** called
Eurasia.

Eiffel Tower in France

Watch a video here!

Europe touches the
Arctic Ocean and the
Atlantic Ocean.

The Alps in Switzerland

Europe has many mountains. The Alps are in the middle of Europe. The Ural Mountains are between Europe and Asia.

MAP OF EUROPE

1. VATICAN CITY
2. SLOVENIA
3. BOSNIA AND HERZEGOVINA
4. MONTENEGRO
5. ALBANIA
6. MACEDONIA

ICELAND

SWEDEN

FINLAND

NORWAY

UNITED KINGDOM

ESTONIA

LATVIA

RUSSIA

DENMARK

LITHUANIA

IRELAND

NETHERLANDS

BELARUS

POLAND

BELGIUM

GERMANY

CZECH REP.

UKRAINE

LUXEMBOURG

SLOVAKIA

LIECHTENSTEIN

ATLANTIC OCEAN

FRANCE

AUSTRIA

HUNGARY

MOLDOVA

2

SWITZERLAND

THE ALPS

CROATIA

ROMANIA

ITALY

3

SERBIA

CORSICA

4

BULGARIA

GEORGIA

1

5 6

SARDINIA

PORTUGAL

SPAIN

SICILY

TURKEY

MEDITERRANEAN SEA

GREECE

CYPRUS

MALTA

The biggest country in Europe is Russia. The smallest is Vatican City. Vatican City is the smallest country in the world. It is in the middle of another country, Italy.

Chapter 2

Mild Climate

The Atlantic Ocean and Mediterranean Sea bring warm temperatures to most of Europe. The **climate** is **mild** in those areas. Northern Europe is colder.

Mediterranean Sea in Greece

Learn more here!

Chapter 3

Plants and Animals

Europe once had many forests. But over time, many trees were replaced with farms and cities.

Madrid, Spain

Learn more here!

Different kinds of bats,
deer, and wolves live in
Europe. Wild boars live
there too.

Northern Europe is home
to polar bears, arctic foxes,
and reindeer.

People of Europe

Each country in Europe has its own people and **culture**. Some countries in northern Europe are known for their fishing businesses.

fishing boats
in Norway

Complete an
activity here!

Italians make a lot of the world's fashion. Many cars are made in Germany.

France is the most visited country in Europe. More than 80 million people visit each year!

Many old buildings
and statues in Europe are
famous. The Colosseum in
Rome, Italy, is an **ancient**
stone **amphitheater**.

Big Ben is a **historic** clock tower in London, United Kingdom.

Making Connections

Text-to-Self

There are many famous buildings and statues in Europe. Would you like to see any of them in real life? Which ones would you like to see?

Text-to-Text

Have you read another book about Europe? What did you learn?

Text-to-World

Europe once had many forests. But over time, forests have been replaced by farms and cities. Why do you think it's important to have forests?

Glossary

amphitheater – an outdoor theater.

ancient – from a long time ago.

climate – temperature and weather of an area.

continent – one of the seven large landmasses on Earth.

culture – beliefs and ways of life of a group of people.

historic – famous or important in history.

landmass – a large area of land.

mild – medium warm, comfortable.

Index

Online Resources

popbooksonline.com

Thanks for reading this Cody Koala book!

Scan this code* and others like it in this book, or visit the website below to make this book pop!

popbooksonline.com/europe

*Scanning QR codes requires a web-enabled smart device with a QR code reader app and a camera.